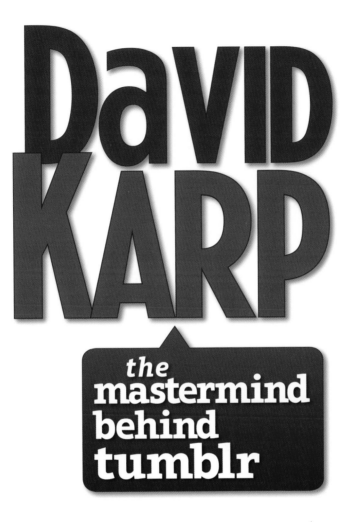

David KARP

the
mastermind
behind
tumblr

KAREN LATCHANA KENNEY

LERNER PUBLICATIONS COMPANY • MINNEAPOLIS

For Nicholson, my personal technology guru

Lerner Publications Company
A division of Lerner Publishing Group, Inc.
241 First Avenue North
Minneapolis, MN U.S.A. 55401

Website address: www.lernerbooks.com

The images in this book are used with the permission of: © Don Emmert/AFP/Getty Images, pp. 2, 26; © Guy Calaf/Bloomberg via Getty Images, p. 6; © http://project.ioni.st/, p. 8; © Thomas Northcut/Photodisc/Getty Images, p. 10; © iStockphoto.com/GYI NSEA, p. 11; © Robert Nickelsberg/Getty Images, p. 13; Cuckoo's Nest/Hanna Barbera/Wang Films/Kobal Collection/Art Resource, NY, p. 14; © Chester Higgins Jr./The New York Times/Redux, pp. 15, 17, 29, 34; © Jim.henderson/Wikimedia Commons, p. 16; © Toshifumi Kitamura/AFP/Getty Images, p. 18; AP Photo/Paul Sakuma, p. 20; Tobias Hase/Picture-Alliance/Newscom, p. 21; Independent Picture Service, pp. 22, 24, 30, 31; © Joe Corrigan/Stringer/Getty Images, p. 27; © Rabbani and Solimene Photography/Stringer/Getty Images, p. 33; © Nadine Rupp/Stringer/Getty Images, p. 36; AP Photo/PRNewsfoto, p. 38; © Ramin Talaie/CORBIS, p. 39.

Front cover: © Don Emmert/AFP/Getty Images.

Main body text set in Rotis Serif Std 55 Regular 13.5/17. Typeface provided by Adobe Systems.

Library of Congress Cataloging-in-Publication Data

Kenney, Karen Latchana.
    David Karp : the mastermind behind Tumblr / by Karen Latchana Kenney.
        p.   cm. — (Gateway biographies)
    Includes bibliographical references and index.
    ISBN 978-1-4677-1285-9 (lib. bdg. : alk. paper)
    1. Karp, David, 1986– 2. Web site development industry—New York (State)—New York—Biography—Juvenile literature. 3. Computer programmers—New York (State)—New York—Biography—Juvenile literature. 4. Young businesspeople—New York (State)—New York—Biography. 5. Tumblr (Electronic resource)—History—Juvenile literature. 6. Entrepreneurship—New York (State)—New York—Juvenile literature. 7. Internet industry—New York (State)—New York—Biography—Juvenile literature. I. Title.
    HD9696.82.U63N49 2013
    338.7'61006752092—dc23 [B]   2012038057

Manufactured in the United States of America
1 – DP – 12/31/12

CONTENTS

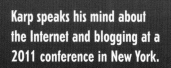

Karp speaks his mind about
the Internet and blogging at a
2011 conference in New York.

The idea had been brewing in David Karp's mind for a year or so. Blogs were such an investment of time. New blogs were being created every day, but many were also abandoned quickly after. The big, blank text box was a little overwhelming to nonwriters. How would they fill it every day? What would they write about? It was a commitment to maintain and update a blog. Not everyone was up for that.

A shorter form of blogging would be better, Karp thought. And a flexible form with a simple, sleek design would be even better—one that could include a photo, a video, a chat, a song or an audio clip, or a short message. What Karp was really thinking about was a tumblelog, a type of short-form blog that is much more than Twitter and far less than Facebook.

Karp had been inspired by a tumblelog called project.ioni.st. It was a blog that was about *sharing*, not publishing. Its editors put up whatever they thought was cool: a quote from Oscar Wilde, a song by Nina Simone,

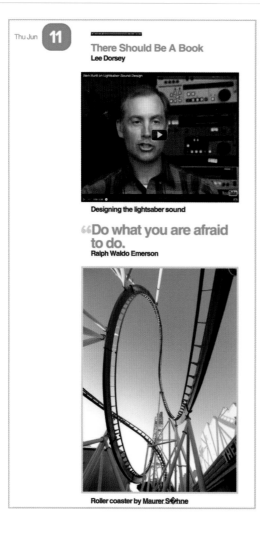

Thu Jun 11

There Should Be A Book
Lee Dorsey

Ben Burtt on Lightsaber Sound Design

Designing the lightsaber sound

"**Do what you are afraid to do.**
Ralph Waldo Emerson

Roller coaster by Maurer Söhne

a photograph of a sea creature by Paul Nicklen. It was like an online scrapbook of what interested the editors the most. Looking through it gave the reader a peek into the editors' thoughts, interests, and experiences. "Little or no commentary was needed. The only context was the author. How absolutely beautiful," Karp wrote.

Karp had been building his own tumblelog for six months. He tweaked it and worked out the bugs. And then he realized: the blog tools he created wouldn't be that hard to make available for others to use. So when there was a two-week lull in Karp's Web consultant business in October 2006, he decided to go for it. He would build a tumblelog that could be used by the masses. It would be just what he wanted in a tumblelog—one spot on the Internet where people could post any type of media they wanted. And maybe, just maybe, it would catch on with other tumbleloggers too. He and developer Marco Arment, Karp's business partner, created the first version of Tumblr in those two weeks. They launched their site in February 2007, showed it to the tumblelog community, and had thirty thousand registered users overnight. Two weeks later that number had grown to seventy-five thousand— and week after week, it just kept growing.

The Coding Kid

David Karp was born on July 6, 1986, in New York City, New York, to parents Michael Karp and Barbara Ackerman. His father is a well-known music composer for television and film. David's mother is a first-grade science teacher at the progressive Calhoun School in Manhattan. David has a younger brother, Kevin, who's a college student at the State University of New York (SUNY) at Stony Brook. The two brothers grew up in the Upper West Side of Manhattan with their parents, who later separated.

From the age of three, David went to the Calhoun School, where his mother taught. He was a good student but did not excel in any particular subject. He was always interested in technology, though. "He was a child who, even at a very young age, knew what he wanted to be," said David's mother. "He was very focused, very driven."

Manhattan's Upper West Side, where David grew up, lies just beyond Central Park.

Before he was even ten years old, David was coding programs on his dad's Apple computer. After school each day, David dialed up and joined America Online (AOL) chat rooms. They were some of the first popular chat rooms on the Internet in the 1990s. At that time, you had to dial up a connection to the Internet through your phone line. It was slow and a bit clunky, but it was also a brand-new way to connect with others. Users had screen names and joined a chat room to communicate with other people—some they knew and some they didn't. David's whole class would be in an AOL chat room. They would instant message one another and e-mail photos back and forth. It was fun, and it made David feel connected with his classmates. "Those were the best times I ever had on the Web," David later said.

Two Idols: Making Magic

Growing up, David said he had two idols—Steve Jobs and Willy Wonka. Jobs was the cofounder of Apple Inc. and a personal computer pioneer. But he was also an inspiring and compelling keynote speaker. During many of his famous keynotes, Jobs revealed new Apple technology, such as the iPod and the iPad. Many of these products went on to become wildly popular. As David grew up, he was "obsessed with Steve Jobs keynotes" and the "show and presentation of the reveal."

And what about Willy Wonka? Wonka is an eccentric

fictional character in the book *Charlie and the Chocolate Factory.* He has an amazing factory that creates unique candy— kinds that no one else ever dreamed of making. "It's sort of the same as Steve, I think—the idea that there is this magical factory, where there's this extraordinary stuff and you can't even begin to conceive what went into creating these things," David explained.

Steve Jobs, one of David's idols, reveals the iPod Touch at a 2007 Apple event.

In 1997, at the age of eleven, David read the book *HTML for Dummies*, taught himself more about coding, and learned how to build Web pages. Soon, he was building websites for local businesses. "I would run around the neighborhood building little storefront websites," he later remembered. He was doing what he loved doing—coding—and he was getting paid for it.

Inside Frederator Studios

Around eighth grade, David started getting a little restless at the Calhoun School. He had to find a new school, since Calhoun only went up to ninth grade. David decided that he wanted to be with a more academic crowd. So he took the science high school test in New York to get into a science school. He got into the Bronx High School of Science. It's a difficult school to get into, but David earned his way in. He attended for his freshman year, but he didn't love it there. He wasn't very engaged with his classes, teachers, or other students. Then that summer David landed an internship that would change his life.

It was at Frederator Studios, an animation production company that was partly focused on the Web. Fred Seibert founded Frederator Studios in 1998. He is the former president of Hanna-Barbera Cartoons who also helped launch MTV in 1981. His company makes cartoons for television, movies, and the Internet. David got the internship in a kind of random way. Seibert's children

The Bronx High School of Science is an elite public school in New York. David was accepted there for his freshman year.

attended the Calhoun School, and his wife ended up talking with David's mom one day. She told Siebert's wife about David's interest in the Internet and coding. Seibert's wife told David's mom about what her husband did. She suggested that David come hang out with her husband at his office. David eventually did. It was a cool place, with red walls and skateboard decks up as art. David was nervous, but Seibert could tell he was into the Internet and coding. The result was an internship.

He was only fourteen when he started his internship, and he was painfully shy. "He couldn't quite look you in the eye," Seibert said. But David was confident when it came to coding. Seibert never knew what David was talking about, but the coders and engineers who worked for Seibert did. Seibert was impressed. And

David liked being around people older than himself. That summer he got his first programming job. It was a project called Secret Goldfish. It would be a private social network for students who had been invited to join. David and the other coders experimented with simple blogging platforms, bookmarking tools, and social recommendations. David wasn't yet great at programming, but he liked it and knew he would get better.

David's parents noticed how much he liked his internship. At the end of that summer, David was messing around on his computer one day. His mom came into the room to talk with him. She asked David how he felt about going back to school that fall. She knew the answer before she asked the question: he was not thrilled about it. Then David's mom proposed something he never expected. What did he think about not going back to school? Instead, she suggested that David be homeschooled by

David has loved working with computers ever since he was young. His mother realized he was passionate and driven and encouraged him to follow his own path.

tutors. And with a flexible school schedule, he could continue his internship. For David, the answer was simple: yes! It was an unconventional path, but it fit David's needs well. "I was getting to work on real projects, not homework. I was getting to build things that would get launched and that people were using. . . . It was an amazing feeling," David remembered.

UrbanBaby and Tokyo

During his internship, David was homeschooled by tutors to continue his education. He took Japanese language classes at the Japan Society on 47th Street in Manhattan. He also bought the domain for davidville.com.

David studied Japanese at the Japan Society, a center for learning about Japanese culture.

When David was sixteen, a fortunate call came into Frederator Studios from a friend of Seibert. He had a site called UrbanBaby that was starting to explode. It was a New York parenting site that had been featured on the TV show *Good Morning America*. It could not handle the Web traffic it was then receiving. The owner, John Maloney, asked Seibert if one of his programmers could help. The call was directed to David, and he did what he could to sort out the site's databases. Then David started working part-time for UrbanBaby.

After a few weeks, Maloney asked David to come on full-time and David agreed. David hadn't even met Maloney in person. Maloney didn't know that David was only sixteen, either. But it was the first real job that David had. He was no longer an intern. He was now a chief technology officer. It would be the start of a three-year working relationship.

At this time, David was still living at home with his parents. And he had teenage friends and a girlfriend who kept him grounded. David worked for UrbanBaby remotely and saved his earnings.

Then, when he was about seventeen, David experienced a life change that left him looking to do something different. His girlfriend of a few years broke up with him. He was heartbroken and felt he had to get out of New York—even though he hadn't finished high school. A new service called Vonage would let David use his New York

John Maloney, former owner of UrbanBaby, offered David a job when he was only sixteen.

phone number through the Internet from anywhere in the world. That meant he could work for UrbanBaby from any location. So he moved to Tokyo, Japan.

While in Japan, David studied and practiced coding. "I was holed up in the middle of this world where it was just me on the Internet," David said. The people at UrbanBaby had no idea David wasn't in New York. "UrbanBaby is calling me at 4 A.M. Tokyo time with tech questions. After three months, they finally caught on that I wasn't in New York. Then they found out that I was seventeen," David later said. Luckily, UrbanBaby didn't care about David's age.

David moved to Tokyo *(above)* as a teen and worked for UrbanBaby from there.

During his time in Tokyo, David decided that he wanted to be an entrepreneur. He started trying to find clients, but he was nervous about sounding young on the phone. "I was so silly—I tried to be very formal and put on a deep voice to clients over the phone so I didn't have to meet them and give away how young I was," he said. "I lied about my age. I lied about the size of my team. I lied about my experience. I was so terribly embarrassed about it for so long. I should have just owned up."

After five months in Tokyo, David moved back to New York. He had a list of executives he wanted to talk with about his services. And his father had created contracts for him to use. David was still working for UrbanBaby, but he also started his own consultant firm. He called it Davidville.

Welcome to Davidville

UrbanBaby was a big hit on the Internet. New York mothers went online to discuss their parenting joys and troubles on its discussion boards. It became so popular that it got the attention of CNET Networks, a major technology and media company that is publicly traded on the stock market. In May 2006, CNET Networks bought UrbanBaby. Karp had equity (financial stakes) in the company, and it paid off when the company went public. "For the first time, I had some money," Karp said.

With the money, the then nineteen-year-old Karp left UrbanBaby to focus on Davidville. This Web consultant

CNET Networks *(left)* bought UrbanBaby in 2006, and David made money in the deal.

company worked on a mix of original projects and projects for clients. Karp put an ad on Craigslist to find an engineer to work for his company. He was a little anxious about it, though. "What do I do when someone actually responds to this thing?" he later said. "I have to, like, meet this person."

The person who responded was Marco Arment. He was two years out of college and had a computer science degree. Karp convinced Seibert to help him interview Arment. And during the interview, Arment wasn't sure who would be his boss. Karp offered the job to Arment. Arment had another offer from Bloomberg—a big financial information and services company. But he chose the position at Davidville instead.

Karp and Arment rented a space in Seibert's studio for their office. Some of the first sites they built were senduit.com and worldwidefido.com, a "YouTube for dogs."

Senduit.com was a file-sharing site that they launched in February 2007. Both were successful sites. In fact, just two months after senduit.com was launched, it was getting 250,000 hits a month. Sixty-five thousand files were being downloaded each month as well.

But it was another of Davidville's sites that would become bigger than either Karp or Arment had imagined. It was the site that Karp had made for his own blogging needs—the one that during a two-week lull in business, Karp and Arment developed further so that it could be used by others. This beta site was the first crude version of Tumblr.

Marco Arment *(above)* **worked for Davidville, David's Web consultant business.**

Hello, Tumblr

Tumblr's first live version was launched in February 2007. It was different from other blogs right from the beginning. It did not have a traditional blog dashboard with text-editing tools. Instead, it had six big buttons with illustrated icons. The icons went with the type of post you could choose from: text, photo, video, link, and dialogue. It had a clean, simple, and modern design. And users could make their Tumblr site completely unique. This site was made to be hacked.

"The one really cool thing was we could let you change anything about its theme," said Karp. "It was just a big chunk of code you could rip apart and make

Tumbleloggers started signing up for Tumblr soon after it launched in early 2007.

original. And it attracted this spectacular community of designers and hackers. Over the next few weeks, they built gorgeous things on Tumblr that didn't look like anything else on the Internet."

The first people who signed up for Tumblr were not the people who had their own independent tumblelogs. They were the people who followed those tumblelogs but didn't know how to create their own. They were a creative bunch interested in how their Tumblr sites looked. Tumblr was attractive to them because it was a new format to play with. And it allowed users to have an incredible amount of design control. Two weeks after it launched, Tumblr had seventy-five thousand users.

In the months following Tumblr's launch, Karp and Arment added new features and tweaked the site's functions. Users' questions were catalysts for the site's development. Karp and Arment kept a blog on WordPress to update users on what was being developed for Tumblr. They also posted notices about the issues the site was having. Users made comments on the blog and also e-mailed Tumblr directly. Karp and Arment listened to what users had to say: both their issues and their praises. And they responded to the needs of the users. Users wanted to communicate with other users. Could they tag photos? They also wanted to see other Tumblr sites.

By the end of March, Tumblr was receiving one hundred e-mails a day from users. Karp found it hard to keep up with all the questions that were coming in. But he and Arment did what they could to keep their users happy.

I ♥♥ **Charts**   Chartists In Residence

7 sets Venn Diagram

128 color combinations from mixing 7 colors

The wide variety of designs on Tumblr sites express their users' personalities. The popular and expressive Tumblr site above evolved into a book called *I Love Charts*.

Some of the changes made in response included new custom themes, new ways to post videos and quotes, and ways to see other users' Tumblr sites. Karp appreciated the users' comments. "It's really easy to build neat things when we know we're building them for our users," he said. He also highlighted some of the cool Tumblr sites that users were building.

The site was gaining users. It was also getting attention from the media. It was mentioned in a *Chicago Tribune* article titled "Is Small Talk the Next Big Thing?" It was also featured on the Lifehacker website. With all the attention came more users and traffic. It was a lot for a two-person team to handle.

Growing Pains

In April 2007, Karp and Arment revealed that the 2.0 version of Tumblr was on its way. It was released on April 27. The new version of Tumblr was more social. It let users follow their friends' sites. The social aspect was found behind the scenes. The dashboard is where Tumblr users connect. Users could now follow other Tumblr blogs. New posts from those blogs showed up in a feed on the dashboard.

Davidville was still the company that put out Tumblr. Karp wanted to continue his consulting work and run Tumblr at the same time. But Tumblr had grown to be a full-time job. The site had grown to having 110,000 users.

By April 2007, Tumblr was already on its way to becoming the major company it is today. Here Karp poses near some of the company's current staff.

The consulting business had to go. In October, Davidville shut down the consulting part of its business. Then the company's name was changed to Tumblr, Inc. Now Karp and Arment could just focus on the needs of the Tumblr site and its users.

That same month, some new partners joined the company too. Karp sold 25 percent of the company for $750,000 to a small group of investors. That group included Bijan Sabet of Spark Capital, Brad Burnham and Fred Wilson of Union Square Ventures, betaworks head

John Borthwick, Vimeo founder Jakob Lodwick, Etsy board member Albert Wenger, and entrepreneur Martin Varsavsky. Plus, Karp's dad and his mentor, Fred Seibert, got in on the company as well. It was now valued at $3 million, just nine months after it was first launched. It was an exciting time for Karp, but it was also a little terrifying for someone so young.

In November, Tumblr 3.0 came out. It had more than four hundred new features and a new interface. And there was now a new type of media that could be posted. The seventh button was added on the dashboard. It was for audio posts. But there was still no way to comment on

Bijan Sabet *(far left)*, an early Tumblr investor, participates in a tech conference in 2011.

other people's posts. Tumblr was working on it, but Karp and Arment still did not know what to do. They didn't like the traditional format of comments on other social media sites. So they continued working on a different way to comment. Soon after its launch, a few bugs appeared with the version. The bugs were soon fixed, though, and the site was back up and running.

Karp wasn't doing a great job at responding to users' support e-mails. He was too busy. Karp had to now do interviews with journalists, write articles and blog posts, and plan feature releases. Karp wanted to be hands-on though and tried to personally respond to Tumblr users. But "it really didn't work and at some point it was getting really bad for the service and it was driving me insane," Karp said.

One user noticed early on. Marc LaFountain was one of the first three thousand Tumblr users. He wrote to the support e-mail address, stating that the company needed a community manager to answer technical questions from users. He offered his help. But Karp wasn't sure that he wanted to grow the Tumblr team. "I thought that hiring one more person we were suddenly gonna go to, like, a team of five or more people, which was just a horrible idea at the time," he later said. But one day Karp faced an in-box of about one thousand unanswered e-mails from users. He realized that it had become too much for him to handle. He called LaFountain up and asked him to start immediately. It was part-time at first, but four months later, LaFountain was the third full-time

These days, the Tumblr office *(above)* is a bustling and well-established place. But when it first started, the company was a tiny operation with a handful of employees.

employee of Tumblr. Having more than a few employees was something Karp would have to get used to.

Big Changes

Things were changing at Tumblr in 2008. The site was attracting more and more users every day. It had three hundred thousand users in May of that year, and more staff was needed to handle the load. It was obvious that Tumblr was a success, but it was still not making any money. Karp was hesitant about accepting advertisers. He didn't want ads to cheapen the look and feel of the site.

The thought of ads "really turns our stomachs," he said at the time. But the company needed to find ways to make money. They were working on some special features that users would have to buy to enhance their Tumblr sites. Investors later killed the idea, though.

Karp and Arment were releasing new updates to the site nearly every day. They had raised funds for the company. But Karp was neglecting a few important things too: the office and its bills, the investors, finding and hiring new staff, Tumblr's lawyers, and many e-mails in his in-box. Karp needed help getting things in order. He looked to his former boss at UrbanBaby—John Maloney.

In September, Maloney was brought on as the president of Tumblr. He focused on business matters and daily operations. That left Karp better able to focus on Tumblr's design and functionality. Arment focused on the engineering aspects of the site. Their goal was to get more users and keep improving the blogging platform. One added feature came in November. Now users could "like" another user's post by clicking a little heart on the

Tumblr users express approval for Tumblr posts by clicking on the heart icon.

The Tumblr Meetups page helps users meet face-to-face.

dashboard. And if a user wanted to meet the owners of blogs they liked, they could go to Meetups in their area. These were events set up by users in their areas and promoted by Tumblr. It was good for the user community and a great way to grow the company.

A new round of funding came in December from the same group of investors. This time they put in $4.5 million. It was enough to last the company two and a half years. But with more money came more expectations. The investors pushed for some kind of revenue from the company. Karp had his work cut out for him.

In early 2009, Tumblr had 625,000 users. The company launched its fifth version in January. It had a new dashboard design, and it had even more community-focused functions. Its Radar page let users see cool content that other users were posting. And it added a search function so that users could find blogs that fit their interests. In addition, there were tons of new themes.

Soon after, Tumblr acquired an iPhone app called Tumblrette. It allowed users to post to Tumblr with their phones. Tumblr updated the app, renamed it, and released it as a free app. The company continued to release new features throughout 2009. They were still small, but the staff was slowly growing. And the site was getting more hits and users every day.

New Investors and Growth

Karp's company was set to explode. The media loved its twenty-three-year-old chief executive officer. He was becoming a bit of a technology celebrity. Karp was named one of the "Beautiful People of 2010" by *Paper Mag*. He was also named one of the top thirty-five technology innovators under the age of thirty-five by *Technology Review*.

In February, Tumblr celebrated its third birthday. And it hit some other big milestones as well. That month there were 1 billion page views. Tumblr was getting 2 million posts a day. And it was getting fifteen thousand new users every day. Tumblr had come a long way in its short time online.

Tumblr received more funding in April 2010 from its investor group. It was their biggest investment yet—$5 million. In the three rounds of investing, Tumblr had raised $10 million. The investors had let Karp take it slow with his company. They were incredible mentors to Karp during that time. But Karp had dreams of big growth for his company. Tumblr was just a team of twelve at the time, but Karp was now open to growing his staff. "We had greater ambitions," he said. For more growth, Karp

Karp has become a celebrity in recent years. Here he hangs out with Brad Richards of the New York Rangers *(left)* and Olympic swimmer Ryan Lochte *(center)*.

needed more money. He was ready to talk with the big investors in Silicon Valley, California.

Before that could happen, there was a big change at Tumblr. Arment left the company to focus on his own projects. He would stay on as a consultant but would no longer be there full-time. There were also a couple of new major hires: Mark Coatney from *Newsweek* and Derek Gottfrid of the *New York Times.*

In October, Karp and Maloney went to Silicon Valley to talk with investors. The next month they announced their new partner—Sequoia Capital. Tumblr received from

Mark Coatney, shown standing between Karp and John Maloney, left *Newsweek* to join Tumblr in 2010.

$25 to $30 million from their new partner. Now they had the money they needed for the growth Karp wanted.

In 2011 Tumblr expanded outside of New York City. It opened an office in Richmond, Virginia. That's where Marc LaFountain lived and Tumblr's support team was located. Karp and his team also experimented with ways the company could make money. The fashion industry was a big fan of Tumblr. So the company offered to sell paid posts by select bloggers to fashion companies. But the effort did not work. Some companies were even offended by the offer.

They still had little revenue, but Tumblr received another dose of funding in September. The company was now valued at $800 million. They received $85 million in this round. It was time to expand. And it was time to really start making money. Karp was now leading a staff of seventy, but it would grow even larger.

A Fashion Model?

Karp stepped into a new role in August 2011—fashion model. He was featured in a digital fashion campaign for the Japanese clothing store Uniqlo. He starred in a two-minute video talking about Tumblr and how people use it. The campaign, called the "Voices of New York," led up to the opening of a new store in New York City.

Tumbling into the Future

The numbers were impressive. By the end of January 2012, Tumblr was getting 15 billion page views each month. A lot of that growth came from Europe. At a conference in Munich that month, Karp announced that they were focusing on having an international presence. And he said that 2012 would be a "big year for revenue development." Karp also said Tumblr needed to add people to its staff to create those new revenue products. Tumblr would be doing a lot of hiring that year.

Karp discusses Tumblr at the Digital Life Design conference in Munich, Germany, in 2012.

Karp was developing more of an interest in the business side of his company. He also had a strong team of managers at the company. Maloney felt it was time for him to leave Tumblr in Karp's hands. In April he stepped down from being the president but stayed on the company's board of directors. Karp was ready for the responsibility. He said, "I've really gotten a kick out of trying to make running a company as Zen an experience as it can be." Heading up a large staff was something Karp was not prepared for though. "I started having to lead, having to manage people much younger I think than most people," Karp said. He went from managing two people to more than one hundred in just two years.

Karp took the challenge well and stayed true to his vision. He runs the company in his own unique way. He doesn't really keep a schedule, except for board meetings. "People tell me I need an assistant, but I don't want one," he said. Instead, he prefers to have a more organic flow at work. Staff just call one another if they need something. And Karp takes notes in a notebook, with a pen. He doesn't always want to be staring at a computer screen. "Being on computers all the time makes me feel gross," he said.

In May, Tumblr revealed that it would start selling ads on Radar and Spotlight. These two features highlight interesting and new content on Tumblr blogs. The starting price for an ad was $25,000. But Karp didn't want any old online ad. He wanted creative advertising on his site, the kind that was "intended to make you feel something for the brand." The first of these paid ads came out in June—first by fashion company Bottega Veneta. Then Adidas bought a larger monthlong campaign. Tumblr was on its way to becoming a profit-making company.

With its new source of revenue, the future looks bright for Karp's company. It had more than 73 million blogs in September 2012. It had been translated into twelve languages. And it was listed at one of the top twenty websites in the United States by Quantcast, a company that analyzes Web traffic and audiences. So is Karp ready to sell his company and cash in? No way. "I'm much more enchanted with the notion of something that's employing

The well-known logo for Adidas began appearing on Tumblr in 2012.

Karp seems well positioned to lead Tumblr into a bright future.

me in fifteen years rather than something that we flip in a year," he said. With that vision, there seem to be no limits to where Karp will lead Tumblr and its many content curators into the future. One thing is for sure—blogging will never be the same.

IMPORTANT DATES

1986	David Karp is born on July 6 in New York City, New York.
1997	He reads the book *HTML for Dummies* and teaches himself how to build Web pages.
2000	At fourteen he begins interning at Frederator Studios.
2002	He starts coding for UrbanBaby.
2003	He moves to Japan for five months.
2006	UrbanBaby is bought by CNET, and Karp receives some money from the sale. He leaves UrbanBaby to focus on his consulting company, Davidville. He hires Marco Arment to be an engineer for Davidville.
2007	Karp and Arment launch Tumblr. The consulting arm of Davidville is shut down, and the company is renamed Tumblr, Inc. Karp sells 25 percent of his company for $750,000 to a small group of investors.

2008	John Maloney, Karp's former boss at UrbanBaby, is brought on as the president of Tumblr. Tumblr receives $4.5 million from investors.
2009	Tumblr acquires Tumblrette, an iPhone app.
2010	Tumblr receives $5 million from investors. Arment leaves Tumblr to focus on his own projects. Sequoia Capital gives Tumblr $25 to $30 million.
2011	Tumblr opens its Richmond, Virginia, branch. The company receives $85 million in funding.
2012	The first paid ads are released on Tumblr. Maloney steps down as president of the company and Karp assumes the role.

SOURCE NOTES

8   David Karp, "Tumblr—Something We've Always Wanted," *Davidville: An Invention Company* (blog), February 19, 2007, http://davidville.wordpress.com/2007/02/19/tumblr/ (October 4, 2012).

9   Doree Shafrif, "Would You Take a Tumblr with This Man?", *New York Observer*, January 15, 2008, http://observer.com/2008/01 /would-you-take-a-tumblr-with-this-man/2/ (August 23, 2012).

10 Maxim staff, "David Karp Is the Barely Legal Blogfather," *Maxim*, n.d., http://www.maxim.com/funny/david-karp-the -barely-legal-blogfather (August 23, 2012).

11 "(Founder Stories) Tumblr's David Karp: My Heroes Are Steve Jobs and Willy Wonka," interview by Erick Schonfeld, *TechCrunch*, February 24, 2011, http://techcrunch .com/2011/02/24/founder-stories-tumblr-karp-jobs-wonka/ (August 24, 2012).

11 Ibid.

12 Maxim staff, "David Karp Is the Barely Legal Blogfather."

13 Rob Walker, "Can Tumblr's David Karp Embrace Ads Without Selling Out?", *New York Times*, July 12, 2012, http://www .nytimes.com/2012/07/15/magazine/can-tumblrs-david-karp -embrace-ads-without-selling-out.html?_r=1&pagewanted=all (August 24, 2012).

15 "David Karp, Founder, Tumblr," radio interview, *From Scratch*, n.d., http://www.fromscratchradio.com/show/david-karp (August 24, 2012).

18 Josh Halliday, "David Karp, Founder of Tumblr, on Realizing His Dream," *Guardian* (London), January 29, 2012, http://www .guardian.co.uk/media/2012/jan/29/tumblr-david-karp-interview (August 28, 2012).

18   Shafrif, "Would You Take a Tumblr?"

19   Halliday, "David Karp, Founder of Tumblr."

19   Martin, J. Quinn, "The 21-Year-Old Behind a 'Darling' New York Web Startup," *New York Sun*, November 8, 2007, http://www .nysun.com/business/21-year-old-behind-a-darling-new-york -web-startup/66108/ (August 27, 2012).

20   Walker, "Can Tumblr's David Karp Embrace Ads?"

20   Quinn, "The 21-Year-Old."

22–23   Tom Cheshire, "Tumbling on Success: How Tumblr's David Karp Built a £500 Million Empire," *Wiredco.uk*, February 2, 2012, http://www.wired.co.uk/magazine/archive/2012/03/features /tumbling-on-success?page=all (September 19, 2012).

25   David Karp, "Bookmarklet Enhancements," *Davidville: An Invention Company* (blog), February 26, 2007, http://davidville .wordpress.com/2007/02/26/bookmarklet/ (October 4, 2012).

28   Johnny Hugel, "Tumblr Cometh," *RVA News*, January 14, 2011, http://rvanews.com/news/tumblr-cometh/36133 (September 14, 2012).

28   Ibid.

30   Mark Milian, "Tumblr: 'We're Pretty Opposed to Advertising,'" *Los Angeles Times*, April 17, 2010, http://latimesblogs.latimes .com/technology/2010/04/tumblr-ads.html (September 15, 2012).

33   "David Karp, Founder, Tumblr," radio interview, *From Scratch*.

36   Brian Anthony Hernandez, "Tumblr Hits 15 Billion Monthly Pageviews," *Mashable*, January 23, 2012, http://mashable .com/2012/01/23/tumblr-15-billion-pageviews/ (September 15, 2012).

37 Walker, "Can Tumblr's David Karp Embrace Ads?"

37 "David Karp, Founder, Tumblr," radio interview, *From Scratch.*

37 Liz Welch, "The Way I Work: David Karp of Tumblr," *Inc.*, May 31, 2011, http://www.inc.com/magazine/201106/the-way-i-work -david-karp-of-tumblr.html (September 15, 2012).

37 Ibid.

37–38 Walker, "Can Tumblr's David Karp Embrace Ads?"

38–39 Sammy Davis, "So What Do You Do, David Karp Founder of Tumblr?" *Mediabistro*, August 27, 2008, http://www .mediabistro.com/So-What-Do-You-Do-David-Karp-Founder-of -Tumblr-a10281.html (September 15, 2012).

SELECTED BIBLIOGRAPHY

"David Karp, Founder, Tumblr." Radio interview. *From Scratch.* N.d. http://www.fromscratchradio.com/show/david-karp (August 24, 2012).

Halliday, Josh. "David Karp, Founder of Tumblr, on Realizing His Dream." *Guardian* (London), January 29, 2012. http://www.guardian.co.uk/media/2012/jan/29/tumblr-david-karp-interview (August 28, 2012).

Martin, J. Quinn. "The 21-Year-Old Behind a 'Darling' New York Web Startup." *New York Sun*, November 8, 2007. http://www.nysun.com/business/21-year-old-behind-a-darling-new-york-web-startup/66108/ (August 27, 2012).

Shafrif, Doree. "Would You Take a Tumblr with This Man?", *New York Observer*, January 15, 2008. http://observer.com/2008/01/would-you-take-a-tumblr-with-this-man/2/ (August 23, 2012).

Walker, Rob. "Can Tumblr's David Karp Embrace Ads Without Selling Out?", *New York Times*, July 12, 2012. http://www.nytimes.com/2012/07/15/magazine/can-tumblrs-david-karp-embrace-ads-without-selling-out.html?_r=1&pagewanted=all (August 24, 2012).

Welch, Liz. "The Way I Work: David Karp of Tumblr." *Inc.*, May 31, 2011. http://www.inc.com/magazine/201106/the-way-i-work-david-karp-of-tumblr.html (September 15, 2012).

FURTHER READING

BOOKS

Brown, Tracy. *Blogger or Journalist?: Evaluating What Is the Press in the Digital Age.* New York: Rosen, 2013.

Doeden, Matt. *Steve Jobs: Technology Innovator and Apple Genius.* Minneapolis: Lerner Publications Company, 2012.

Firestone, Mary. *Wireless Technology.* Minneapolis: Lerner Publications Company, 2009.

Harris, Ashley Rae. *Facebook: The Company and Its Founders.* Edina, MN: Abdo, 2013.

Hudson, David L. *Blogging.* 2nd ed. New York: Chelsea House, 2011.

Wilkinson, Colin. *Twitter and Microblogging: Instant Communication with 140 Characters or Less.* New York: Rosen Central, 2012.

Woods, Michael, and Mary B. Woods. *Ancient Computing Technology: From Abacuses to Water Clocks.* Minneapolis: Twenty-First Century Books, 2011.

WEBSITES

Crunch Base: David Karp
    http://www.crunchbase.com/person/david-karp
    Visit David Karp's profile page at Crunch Base for basic facts on the young entrepreneur.

David Karp's Tumblelog
    http://www.davidslog.com
    Check out Karp's Tumblelog to see photos, funny and thought-provoking quotes, and other random things that Karp finds interesting.

From Scratch: David Karp
    http://www.fromscratchradio.com/show/david-karp
    Visit this page to listen to a fascinating interview with David Karp.

Tumblr
    http://www.tumblr.com
    Create a Tumblr account or browse others' accounts in a variety of categories, from animals to crafts to celebrities.

INDEX